Why We Need Rainforests

Written by Tess Schembri
Series Consultant: Linda Hoyt

WorldWise™
Content-based Learning

Contents

Introduction

The air around you feels warm and sticky, as if it will rain. You can hear sounds – birds and animals hidden in the trees, and running water. You can see tall trees and strange plants, vines and creepers and flowers. And the smell coming from all the plants and trees and flowers is something that you have never smelt before. What is this amazing place?

It is a **tropical** rainforest.

Many people, animals and plants need rainforests to survive, but sadly, people have now destroyed more than half of the rainforests in the world.

Rainforests are **endangered**.

Chapter 1

Life in rainforests

People in rainforests

For thousands of years, small groups of people have lived in rainforests. They know and use the foods, **medicines**, plants and animals that can be found there, but they are careful to take only what they need.

When a rainforest is destroyed, the people who live there are forced to change their way of life.

Find out more

Are there rainforests in your country? Which countries near where you live have the largest rainforests?

Animals and plants in rainforests

More than half of the reptiles, insects, mammals and birds in the world live in rainforests.

Many kinds of colourful birds are found only in rainforests, while other birds visit rainforests during the year when food and nesting **sites** are to be found there.

More kinds of plants grow in rainforests than anywhere else in the world, and many rainforest plants and animals cannot be found anywhere else.

The animals and plants in rainforests depend on one another for survival. Rainforest animals need plants for food and shelter and many plants need insects to **pollinate** their flowers. They also need animals to spread their seeds.

Macaws

Harpy eagle

Hummingbird

Iguana

Orangutan

9

Rainforest trees

The trees in the rainforest are very important. They give us **rubber**, which can be made into many things, and they also give us wood to make furniture.

Rainforest trees help to stop soil from washing away. The leaves and branches of rainforest trees take in the rain, and their roots hold the soil together.

When rainforests are cut down, heavy rain washes the soil away, so there is not enough for the plants to use. The soil often gets washed into rivers so that the rivers get blocked or change **course**, or sometimes, they overflow and flood the land.

Mahogany trees

Rubber trees

Did you know?

Rainforests cover about 6 per cent of the Earth's surface, but they are home to more than half of the world's plant and animal species.

Chapter 2

How rainforests help us

Foods and medicines

Many of the foods we eat every day come from rainforests – foods such as bananas, pineapples and avocados. There are many other rainforest foods that animals rely on.

If we destroy the rainforests, we also destroy these foods.

Avocados

Did you know?

Brazil nuts come from rainforest trees. They are very good to eat because they provide important nutrients.

Bananas

Many **medicines** are made from rainforest plants.

Some medicines that are used to treat serious illnesses come from these plants. In the future, other rainforest plants might be used to make new medicines that we do not know about yet.

If the rainforests are destroyed, we will not be able to use these plants.

Rainforests and climate

Rainforests help control the earth's temperature.

Cutting down rainforests is changing the earth so that many places that are cold are getting warmer, and places that are warm are getting very hot. Ice in the sea is melting, and some places are flooded, while other places turn into deserts.

Many plants and animals all over the world will die.

Rainforests are called "the lungs of the earth". This is because they release oxygen into the air. We need oxygen to breathe.

Cutting down rainforests changes the climate, causing ice to melt.

Chapter 3

Saving rainforests

Rainforests are cut down so that the land can be used for farming, for mining and to build new roads and houses. People also cut down rainforest trees for timber. Because of this, rivers that run through rainforests can be polluted and people, animals and plants cannot get clean water.

People must stop destroying rainforests. We need to choose to use timber and paper that does not come from rainforests. We should try to live in a way that does not damage the environment.

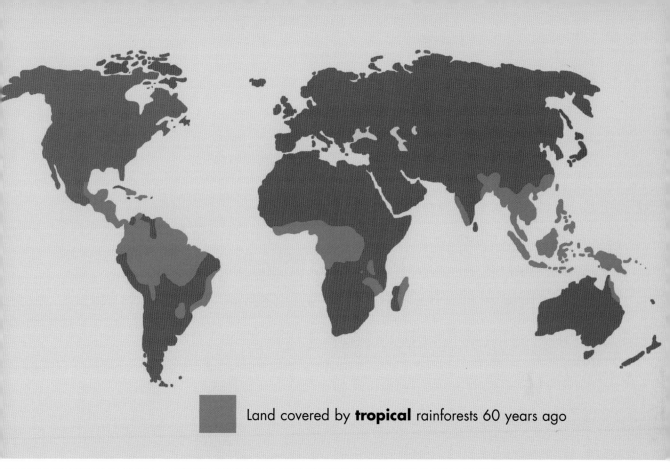

Land covered by **tropical** rainforests 60 years ago

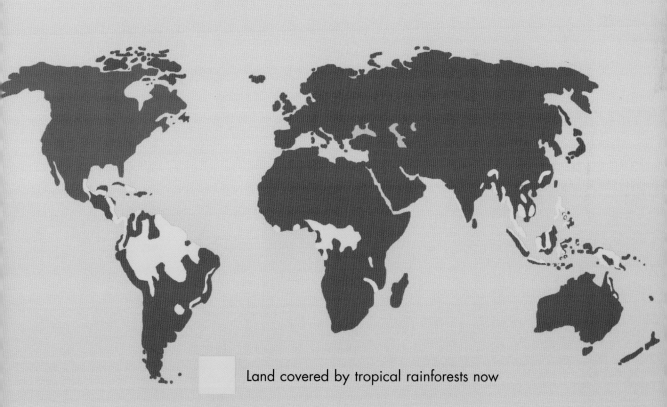

Land covered by tropical rainforests now

Conclusion

People have destroyed more than half of the world's **tropical** rainforests in the past 60 years.

Rainforests cannot be replaced. Once they have been destroyed, they are gone forever, and the plants and animals disappear forever, too.

We must save our rainforests now!

Glossary

course   the natural path where a river flows

endangered   at a high risk of dying out and becoming extinct

medicines   things that can be used to treat illness and disease

pollinate   to take pollen from one plant to another so that new seeds can be made

rubber   a stretchy material that is made from the milky liquid in tropical plants

sites   places where things such as nests are built

tropical   found in the tropics, where the climate is hot and rainy

Index